WILLIE LYNCH

Why African-Americans have so many issues!

by
Marc Sims

Manuscript edited by
Veronica Sorrell
Sorrell Enterprises

WILLIE LYNCH
Why African Americans have so many issues!

By Marc Sims

ISBN # 0-9728043-0-7
Printed in the United States of America

Marc Sims
P.O. Box 5415
Chicago, IL 60680
e-mail address:
willielynch2013@yahoo.com

Special thanks to:

WVON 1450 AM Radio
Chicago
Staff & Listeners

My Family and Friends
in Chicago

TABLE OF CONTENTS

FOREWORD

Some time during the last decade of the 1900s, copies of a speech surfaced in the African American community, said to be an historic address delivered to a group of Virginia slave holders by a West Indian plantation owner named Willie Lynch. Exactly when and how this speech was discovered remains a mystery. Some historians have declared it as authentic without a doubt, while others have proclaimed it a myth or even a hoax.

Regardless of one's opinion, this speech presents a haunting picture of the deliberate, systematic corruption of the African people who were brutally torn from their homes and families and forced to work as slaves in cotton, tobacco, and sugar plantations throughout the Americas.

While U.S. legislators debate the merits of Reparations for the descendants of slaves, psychologists are documenting the many signs of psychological trauma that still exists among African Americans as a result of the not too distant slave experience.

The dysfunctional family is a chronic condition that has been passed down from generation to generation. It has its roots in the deliberate separation of black families during the slave era, in both the North and the South.

Although the origins of the Willie Lynch method of slave repression remain unknown, ironically, nearly every social ill in the African American community can be traced to some aspect of this system presented in Virginia in 1712.

The American institution of slavery was very scientific in its destruction of a people for the purpose of creating a permanent labor force.   But not only have African Americans suffered as a result of slavery. The soul of white America was also destroyed in the process of upholding an evil system that condoned the making of men into mindless beasts.

Africa built its great empires on the strength of a united family and community. Within African languages and customs are constant reinforcements of the system of respect given to elders and the importance of strengthening family ties.   These two strong cultural values had to be destroyed in order for slavery to survive.

It is known that the breakup of the family and the separation of tribes and clans who spoke the same language was essential for the prevention of organized uprisings. The separation of babies from their mothers and fathers at an early age was also a deliberate, systematic means of insuring that the next generation would be ignorant children who were emotionally disconnected from their fore parents.   This tragic condition continues to exist today in African American communities.

As we researched history for our book *Slavery: The African American Psychic Trauma*, we discovered that detailed records of our African ancestors had been carefully preserved – and hidden away in institutions controlled by whites. The Africans who were brought to America and forced into slavery were writers, educators, builders, agricultural experts, religious leaders, and soldiers. This was the story that had never been told in American history books. It was certainly not taught in American schools.

We discovered that many of our African ancestors wrote manuscripts while on the plantation, describing their homes, their families, their culture and their lives prior to the capture and enslavement by whites. Their writings were often in Arabic, the common language used in many African schools and universities. However, their American born children were told the lie that their parents had been ignorant, naked savage people who were fortunate enough to be brought to America by whites to become civilized.

These children, having no access to their fore parents' language or writings, believed the lie, and therefore had no memories of previous independence to help them overcome the effects of slavery. In their own eyes they were a people of little value.

This is an attitude that still exists among their descendants. Consider what is highlighted during Black History Month.

Today, when African American children strive to find something in their history of which to be proud, the best examples they can find are of some courageous black slave. They have no knowledge of the names, faces and stories of African free people that had successful lives before they were captured and forced into slavery. Therefore, in the minds of black children born in America, they are a people who came from slaves.

Empires rise and fall throughout the course of history. People of all nationalities have experienced temporary setbacks due to wars, migrations and other socio-political events. But they always retained a memory of a great history, and these memories gave them faith that one day they would rise again. Not so with African Americans. Never before have a people been so thoroughly beaten down that they seem to have lost the will to ever lift themselves up again.

African American leaders with great oratorical skills rise to prominence with messages of hope for the future. Yet, the knowledge of how to create strong families and communities continues to elude the best of them.

Elected officials have successfully passed legislation designed to reverse some of the damage done by centuries of slavery and decades of racial discrimination thereafter. Yet, new laws have not been able to transform African American communities into well-functioning entities.

Despite a powerful Civil Rights movement that inspired political activists around the world, African Americans still find themselves the perpetual victims of their own self-destructive behavior.   Drugs, crime, violence, and chronically broken homes are plagues that no amount of sit-ins, demonstrations, and boycotts have been able to remove.

What will it take to remove the deeply ingrained self-hatred that took root during slavery and continues to reproduce itself generation after generation?

In this book, renowned talk show host Marc Sims takes a close look at the Willie Lynch speech and its continued affect on the behavior of African Americans. Regardless of how this speech became known to the general public, there comes a point when we as a people must seriously look at our self-destructive behavior. We need to deliberately de-program ourselves in order to end the cycle of mental enslavement.

For many, particularly those who pride themselves on being among the "educated" class, it will be difficult to admit to being duped into a self-perpetuating cycle of failure as a result of not knowing how to cooperate with ones family and neighbors. But each of us must look at our own behavior.

In today's society, as in all successful societies, progress is made only by collective effort. Observe the international power of corporate America. Observe the great African empires of the Middle Ages. Africans built the great Ghana empire by using the same universal principle of cooperation between family groups.

The system introduced by Willie Lynch was designed to keep African Americans from ever again forming the strong family groups that led to the creation of the Ghana empire. It was designed to keep them so petty, childish, selfish, and jealous of each other that they could never join forces for mutual advancement.

The unfortunate reality is that the conditions that exist in the African American community can only be resolved through a collective, unified effort. This is why we must acknowledge the deliberate psychological damage inflicted upon us over the past few centuries. We must methodically undo the self-perpetuating system of destructive disunity introduced in 1712 to perpetuate control over Blacks by White enslavers.

Read this book. Examine yourself. Then consciously strive to reverse the brainwashing process.

We must not let Willie Lynch prevail.

Sultan Abdul Latif and
Naimah Latif
Co-authors
Slavery: The African American
Psychic Trauma

THE WILLIE LYNCH SPEECH

Gentlemen, I greet you here on the bank of the James River in the year of our Lord, one thousand seven hundred and twelve. First, I shall thank you, the gentlemen of the Colony of Virginia, for bringing me here. I am here to help you solve some of your problems with slaves. Your invitation reached me on my modest plantation in the West Indies where I have experimented with some of the newest and still the oldest methods for control of slaves. Ancient Rome would envy us if my program is implemented.

As our boat sailed south on the James River, named for our illustrious King, whose version of the Bible we cherish, I saw enough to know that your problem is not unique. While Rome used cords of wood as crosses for standing human bodies along its old highways in great numbers, you are using the tree and the rope on occasion.

I caught the whiff of a dead slave hanging from a tree a couple of miles back. You are not only losing valuable stock by hangings, you are having uprising, slaves are running away, your crops are sometimes left in the fields too long for maximum profit, you suffer occasional fires, your animals are killed. Gentleman, you know what your problems are; I do not need to elaborate. I am not here to enumerate your problems; I am here to introduce you to methods of solving them.

In my bag here, I have a foolproof method for controlling your black slaves. I guarantee every one of you that if installed correctly it will control the slaves for at least 300 years. My method is simple; any member of your family or any overseer can use it. I have outlined a number of differences among the slaves, and I take these differences and make them bigger. I use fear, distrust, and envy for control purposes. These methods have worked on my modest plantation in the West Indies, and it will work throughout the South.

Take this simple little list of differences and think about them. On top of my list is "Age" but it is there only because it starts with "A", the second is "Color" or shade, there is intelligence, size, sex, size of plantations, status on plantation, attitude of owners, whether the slaves live in the valley, on a hill, East, West, North, South, have fine hair or coarse hair, or is tall or short.

Now that you have a list of differences, I shall give you an outline of action; but before that I shall assure you that distrust is stronger than trust, and envy is stronger than adulation, respect, or admiration.

The black slave, after receiving this indoctrination, shall carry on and will become self-refueling and self-generating for hundreds of years, maybe thousands.

Don't forget, you must pit the old black male vs. the young black male, and the young black male against the old black male. You must use the dark skin slaves vs. the light skin slaves, and the light skin slaves vs. the dark skin slaves. You must use the female vs. the male, and male vs. the female. You must also have all your white servants and overseers distrust all blacks but it is necessary that your slaves trust and depend on us. They must love, respect and trust only us.

Understanding is the best thing. Therefore, we shall go deeper into this area of the subject matter concerning what we produced here in this breaking process of the female nigger. We have reversed the relations. In her natural uncivilized state she would have a strong dependency on the uncivilized nigger male, and she would have a limited protective tendency toward her independent male offspring and would raise the female offspring to be dependent like her. Nature has provided for this type of balance.

We reversed nature by burning and pulling one uncivilized nigger apart and bull whipping the other to the point of death, all in her presence. By her being left alone, unprotected, with the male image destroyed, the ordeal caused her to move from her psychological dependent state to a frozen independent state. In the frozen psychological state of independence she will raise her male and female offspring in reverse roles. For fear of the young male's life, she will psychologically train him to be mentally weak and dependent but physically strong.

Because she has become psychologically independent, she will train her female offspring to be psychologically independent. What you got? You've got the nigger woman out front and the nigger man behind and scared.

This is a perfect situation for sound sleep and economics. Before the breaking process, we had to be alertly on guard at all times. Now we can sleep soundly for, out of frozen fear, his woman stands guard for us, he cannot get past her early infant slave molding process. He is a good tool, now ready to be tied up to the horse at a tender age.

By the time a nigger boy reaches the age of sixteen, he is soundly broken in and ready for a long life of sound and efficient work and the reproduction of a unit of good labor force.

Continually, through the breaking of uncivilized savage niggers, by throwing the nigger female savage into a frozen psychological state of independency, by killing of the protective male image, and by creating a submissive dependent mind in the nigger male savage, we have created an orbiting cycle that turns on its own axis forever, unless a phenomenon occurs and re-shifts the position of the male and female savages.

We show what we mean by example. Take the case of low economic slave units and examine them closely.

We breed two nigger males with two nigger females. Then we take the nigger males away from them and keep them moving and working. Say the one nigger female bears another nigger female and the other bears a nigger male. Both nigger females, being without influence of the nigger male image, frozen with an independent psychology, will raise their offspring into reverse positions. The one with the female offspring will teach her to be like herself, independent and negotiable (we negotiate with her, through her, by her, and negotiate at her will).

The one with the nigger male offspring, she being frozen with a subconscious fear for his life, will raise him to be mentally dependent and weak, but physically strong, in other words, body over mind. Now, in a few years when these two offspring's become fertile for early reproduction, we will mate and breed them and continue the cycle. That is good, sound, and long range comprehensive planning.

Earlier we talked about the non-economic good of the horse and the nigger in their wild or natural state; we talked about the principle of breaking and tying them together, of the savage and her offspring for the orderly future planning; then, more recently we stated that by reversing the positions of male and female savages we had created an orbiting cycle that turns on its own axis forever, unless a phenomenon occurred and re-shifted the positions of the male and female savages.

Our experts warned us about the possibility of this phenomenon occurring, for they say that the mind has a strong drive to correct and re-correct itself over a period of time if it can touch some substantial original historical base; and they advised us that the best way to deal with this phenomenon is to shave off the brute's mental history and create a multiplicity of phenomenon of illusions, so that each illusion will twirl in its own orbit, something similar to floating balls in a vacuum.

This creation of a multiplicity of phenomena of illusions entails the principles of crossbreeding divisions of labor, the results of which is the severance of the points of the original beginnings for each sphere illusion. Since we feel that the subject matter may get more effective when cross breeding horses and niggers, we shall lay down the following definitional terms for future generations:

- *Orbiting cycle means a thing in a given path.*
- *Axis means upon which or around which a body turns.*
- *Phenomenon means something beyond ordinary conception that inspires awe and wonder.*
- *Multiplicity means a great number.*
- *Sphere means globe.*
- *Cross-breeding a horse means taking a horse and breeding it with an ass and you get a dumb backwards ass longhead mule that is not reproductive and nonproductive by itself.*
- *Cross-breeding niggers means taking so many drops of good white blood and putting them into as many*

nigger women as possible, varying the drops by the various tones that you want, and then letting them breed with each other until the circle of colors appear as you desire.

What this means is this: Put the niggers and the horses in the breeding pot, mix some asses and some good white blood and what do you get? You get a multiplicity of colors of ass backward, unusual niggers, funning, tied to backward ass longhead mules, the one productive of itself, the other sterile. One is constant and the other dying. We keep the nigger constant for we may replace the mule with another tool. Both mule and nigger tied to each other, neither knowing where the other came from and neither productive for itself, nor without each other.

Cross breeding completed. For further severance from their original beginning, we must completely annihilate the mother tongue of both the new nigger and the new mule and institute a new language that involves the new life's work of both. You know, language is a particular institution. It leads to the heart of a people. The more a foreigner knows about the other country, the more he is able to move through all levels of that society.

Therefore, if the foreigner is an enemy of another country, to the extent that he knows the body of the language, to that extent is the country vulnerable to attack or invasion of a foreign culture. For example, you take a slave, if you teach him all about your language, he will know all your secrets, and he is then no more a slave, for you can't fool him any longer, and being a fool is one of the basic ingredients of and to the maintenance of the slavery system.

For example, if you told a slave that he must perform in getting out "our crops" and he knows the language well, he would know that "our crops" didn't mean "our" crops and the slavery system would break down, for he would relate on the basis of what "our crops" really meant. So you have to be careful in setting up the new language for the slaves would soon be in your house, talking to you as "man to man" and that is a death to our economic system. In addition, the definition of words or terms is only a minute part of the process.

Values are created and transported by communication through the body of the language to connect them from orderly working in the society. A total society has many interconnected value systems. All these values in the society have bridges of language to connect them for orderly working in the society. But for these language bridges, these many value systems would clash and cause internal strife or civil war, the degree of the conflict being determined by the magnitude of issues or relative opposing strength in whatever form.

For example, if you put a slave in a hog pen and train him to live there and incorporate him to value it as a way of life completely, the biggest problem you would have out of him is that he would worry you about provisions to keep the hog pen clean, or partially clean or he might not worry you at all. On the other hand, if you put this same slave in the same hog pen and make a slip and incorporate something in his language whereby he comes to value a house more than he does a hog pen, you got a problem. He will soon be in your house.

Gentlemen, these kits are your keys to control, use them. Have your wives and children use them. Never miss an opportunity. My plan is guaranteed, and the good thing about this plan is that if used intensely for one year, the slaves themselves will remain perpetually distrustful.

INTRODUCTION

This book is about African Americans, a very complicated people. African Americans are a conquered and divided people. We are an amalgam of bloodlines and cultures. Black Africans were bought to the "new world" as slaves for the white man. Our ancestors were stripped of their original names, religion, and culture. Then they endured 300 years of chattel slavery. If that wasn't enough, our great-grandparents, grandparents, and parents endured 100 years of segregation, discrimination, injustice, and inequality!

Now the descendents of the slaves are free! We are now free to act like fools! We are free to spend our money anywhere, and any way our little hearts desire. More than ever before, we can live almost anywhere we want, and go to school anywhere we want. But the freedom to assimilate into the world of European Americans has also caused African Americans so many problems!

Visit any city in the United States of America and you will find African Americans residing in the "bad" part of town. Why is this? Why are there so many African American men unemployed? Why do some African American men commit so many murders, perpetrate so many street crimes, and abandon their children? There are many "good" African American men, but where are they? Are they in the suburbs? Are they in church? Or are they all living with white women?

African Americans have numerous problems and challenges that impede our progress. We have to deal with institutional racism, modern day capitalism, and the constant vilification of low income African Americans by the media. There are other problems, but the worst one we have to deal with is our own self-hatred! You can thank Mr. Lynch for starting the process and today's white and black leaders for continuing the process of divide and conquer.

Today there are millions of African Americans who don't like being black, and we all have some degree of disdain for each other. Anyone can find reasons not to like someone, but some African Americans look for reasons not to like other African Americans.

We must come to the cold hard reality that the white man is at the root of all of our problems. Yes, we must blame "the white man." We must blame Willie Lynch.

Mr. Lynch was a very wise slave owner who gave a speech instructing other white slaves owners on how to control their slaves. Willie Lynch gave the slave owners his foolproof method and said it could last for three hundred years. Willie Lynch had a divide and conquer strategy of pitting the black man against the black woman. It worked then and it is working today! All of Mr. Lynch's other strategies are also working today.

The authenticity of the Willie Lynch speech is really irrelevant because the strategy to divide and conquer works. It is the oldest trick in the book of tricks because it works so well. It takes a conscious, emotionally sound individual to resist the power of a divide and conquer plot. You need to have a real understanding of world history and believe in sound principles and values to be able to withstand a divide and conquer tactic.

Ask yourself why African Americans are so divided? Why do we like white people and their world more than we love our community? Why are 70% of African American children born out of wedlock? Why are there so many single African American women? Why are there more African American women in college than African American men? Why is HIV and Aids a growing problem for young African Americans?

Why do all African Americans receive inferior health care? The issues we have go on and on!

You can go anywhere in this country and see black men dating, marrying, and/or having children with white women. Now you are starting to see more black women openly dating and marrying white men. Why is this?

Why are so many African American women doing very well economically and spiritually, and also why are there so many single, salty, angry, and puffed up sistas?

The slave owner Willie Lynch knew how to divide the slaves and keep their descendants divided. He said his method would last for three hundred years. He was absolutely right! In this modern time, this new millennium, there remain divisions between the young and the old, the dark skin, and the light skin, the male and the female African American.

African Americans are a very confused people, but ironically we have the power to end white supremacy! It is probably our destiny. It is probably why the Willie Lynch's of the past and present work so hard to pit African Americans against other.

Was there a divine reason why African slaves suffered 300 years of chattel slavery? Was there a divine reason why the descendents of African slaves suffered 100 years of hell?

Maybe Willie Lynch knew something, and maybe today's "powers that be" know something. They know a unified African American community would conquer white supremacy. The institutions of the United States of American purposely lure African Americans in front of a television screen or a movie screen, and away from a library or a bookstore. They also lure us away from each other!

EDUCATION

"The black slave, after receiving this indoctrination, shall carry on and will become self-refueling and self-generating for hundreds of years, maybe thousands."

Willie Lynch

There is an old saying used many times on WVON radio station in Chicago: "You cannot expect white people to teach black children to compete with white children." Year after year the average African American parents send their children to inferior public schools. The public schools and private schools turn African American children, especially boys, into "Negroes" or "niggers."

This may sound very harsh until you analyze the results. For the purpose of this argument, the controversial word nigger means an uncouth person. There are millions of niggers in America.

A few may live on your block, or down the street. In urban black America, they seem to be everywhere. There is a not-so-old saying that is also true: "Niggers don't die, they multiply!" Negroes are everywhere too! Negroes are African Americans who want to be white or want to be accepted by whites as equals.

Most educators would be considered Negroes. They are well-intentioned people, but they have been mentally conditioned by a white, supremacist American culture. We have all been affected by Willie Lynch! Willie Lynch's divide and conquer tricks have African American men, women, and children at odds with each other today.

Every African American student should read the Willie Lynch speech before they leave elementary school and reexamine the speech before they complete high school. The Willie Lynch speech should be taught in school, in the home, and in every religious and community organization.

The reason for teaching students the Willie Lynch speech is to eventually eliminate negroism and niggerism. The purpose is to end the three hundred year spell of Willie Lynch. When adults and children know better, they tend to do better.

The educational system and popular culture of the United States turn African American children into mentally dead human beings. In elementary school, most African American children are inadequately educated. Some African Americans are adequately educated, a few are fully educated, but all are mis-educated by the omission of real history. What African American students received is "His-story"! Yes, the "white man's", or a European version of world history.

Just remember your history lessons about the United States of America. It is a very impressive history! Especially when you compare it with African American history. The African slaves served their white slave masters for three hundred years. Then the freed slaves and their descendants had to deal with one hundred years of discrimination and injustice.

The whites slowly but surely used the free labor of black African slaves to build a paradise in North America. Historic honors should be given to the whites that founded the United States because they were brave and great men of determination and vision.

However, we must not forget that some of these great men were slave owners! The black African men, women, and children were not equal to white men. Nor were white women equal to the white men. Nor were the indigenous people, called Indians, considered equal to them.

These simple historical facts are cracks in the foundation of the history of the United States. Some of these cracks are being patched up, but many still remain. This is supposed to be a country where there is freedom and justice for all, but the descendants of American Indians and African slaves have never received a full level of freedom and justice.

Our children need to know the truth; the truth will set them free from Willie Lynch! The truth is that the institutions in America are structured to make and keep African Americans subservient to European Americans.

Every African American educator is a walking history lesson. They can tell students their life stories and how they relate to the lives of their students. It is to bad too many educators are afraid to give young students a complete history lesson! They are afraid of giving their students a living history lesson because undeniable truth will empower their students.

Educators are afraid of losing their jobs for giving African American students the inspiration to defeat white supremacy. African American students need to be taught how history relates to their lives and their world.

No educator wants to teach black children to hate white people or any one else. However, African American students should have a good education about racism and white supremacy. The institutions of the United States have a history of brain washing and controlling the minds of African Americans.

Our educators have the responsibility of inspiring their students to read. Everything a student wants to know or needs to know is in a book or on the Internet. There are many excellent books and websites to read. Reading will expand a student's mind and prevent him from turning into a thug!

Encouraging a child to read is a challenge. Very few students are born readers. The majority of students have to be inspired. If the love of reading did not start at home, or at pre-school, then the responsibility falls on the elementary school educator.

Some parents also have to be inspired to read. The first book all African American parents and educators must read is Carter G. Woodson's *The Mis-Education of the Negro*.

Every black bookstore is full of mind enlightening books to read and also audiotapes and compact discs to listen to in the car. Continuous learning must become a way of life in the African American community. Parents definitely need to read a book on raising an African American child in this European American dominated society.

Many educators of black children are white. White people, and also black people who think like white people, control the United States' educational systems. Because of this, African American students are not taught to use their education to create businesses and other institutions that would improve life in African American neighborhoods.

African American students are taught, instead, to act as individuals. They are taught to look out for themselves, get a good job, and forget about our people. There are millions of brothers and sisters who have followed this advice and moved as far as they possibly could from our old urban neighborhoods. Moving away from people who have a ghetto mentality is understandable, but instead we need to come on back home and make the public schools one of the institutions that will destroy the ghetto mentality.

African Americans will never eliminate ignorance, street crimes, or poverty until we create a cultural movement for academic excellence. Human beings are influenced by their families, friends, neighbors and their cultures. In low-income neighborhoods there is a culture of survival. There is very little energy and intellect to inspire students to raise their life's expectation beyond survival.

Every child will not grow up to be a rocket scientist, computer scientist, or professional athlete, but every student must be encouraged to believe they can reach a reasonable level of academic success.

This may sound impossible, because the majority of African American children attend inferior public schools. Yes, the average public schools in African American neighborhoods are bad, but it is the responsibility of "the village" to make the schools better. It does not matter how much our local or national politicians say they want to improve the public schools. African Americans should never expect white people to teach black children to compete with white children, so African Americans must have a different mission for the average urban public school. Part of this mission should be to teach African American children to love themselves, other African Americans, and their own neighborhoods.

Wealthy parents can send their children to the best schools! These schools have the best educators, the best curriculums, the best equipment, the best administrators, and the best resources. Middle income and poor African Americans reluctantly send their children to inferior public schools. The rich always get the best, and the poor get what's left!

There could be a much bigger problem for low-income students than inferior public schools. Wealthy and well-educated parents expect the best from and for their children. What do lower income parents expect from and for their children? Subconsciously some low-income parents may not want their children to achieve in school.

Now before you get too upset, just think about it! Children are a reflection of their parent's desires and the child's environment. Subconsciously, some parents may not want their children to excel for fear they will leave them in poverty. Remember, misery loves company!

There are numerous psychologist and other professionals. They should study this theory further. The point is, we are all products of our environment and success or failure is contagious. Any educator will tell you that good students usually are the result of good parenting and bad students usually are the result of bad parenting.

Many of the challenges facing African Americans will be eliminated when public education becomes the top priority of every concerned resident and community organization. Willie Lynch has divided African Americans for three hundred years; it is time for us to put aside our petty differences and save our children!

The next generation of gangbangers, illegal drug addicts and incompetent parents are currently attending inferior public schools. Visit the average public school and you will see the future of the African American community.

African Americans need local and national leaders who will totally focus on the proper education of African American children. Excellent preschools, grammar schools, and high schools are desperately needed in every African American community.

The key to success is creating independent and focused leadership for education. These leaders would put constant pressure on principals, parents, and public school boards. Children are born brilliant, but the public schools do a remarkable job of mentally beating the brilliance out of African American children.

Every African American child has a unique talent. Every child is born with the potential to do something great. It is the responsibility of all African Americans to develop an educational system to bring out and develop those skills.

What are the ingredients of an excellent public school system? We need cooperative parents, children, and public school educators who are working together for the success of the students. What are the components of the average public school in our community?

Subconsciously, some parents may not want their children to achieve in school. If a school is poorly educating students, it is often because the parents are poorly educated and cannot help children with their homework, or unwilling to demand better performance from the children and their children's school.

African Americans will never fully eliminate the ills of our community until all African Americans participate in the betterment of African American children. This cultural movement can quickly turn into a way of life.

Every educator has the power to keep a student either on the right path or on the road to poverty. Educators need the support of their educational system, parents, and community residents. All educational systems should give educators the power to kick out poorly performing, misbehaving students who demonstrate they cannot be reformed.

These students should not be allowed to hold back the student who wants to learn. Special classes or special schools should be set up to help those students with their educational or emotional needs. Also, parents should train their children to be well behaved and ready to learn.

Unruly and disrespectful students are top reasons why the public schools are so bad.   Public school educators should create special programs for these badass children!

Everyone in the United States should also demand higher pay for educators in middle and low-income school districts.

Educators are at their best when they become real, honest and passionate about the subjects they are teaching.   Educators are also at their best when they relate what they are teaching with the reality of their students' world.   They are the most important component in the future success of African Americans.

They need the support of the entire African American community.   Educators need more compensation for their services, more computer equipment, and more help with their unprepared, unruly students.   If African Americans want to eliminate crime and poverty, we need more educational funding and more volunteers for our children.

We are living in the digital age!   With new digital devices and programs popping up all around us, every student should be reading at grade level.   Computers can easily teach a student without a teacher or parent being present.   The writers of computer soft-wear programs will solve the so-called "qualified teacher shortage".

The teachers unions may not like it, but many students will eventually receive a good education via lap top computers, large flat screen monitors, and well-trained human facilitators.

In this digital age, no student should be undereducated or mis-educated!

BLACK WOMEN

"By her being left alone, unprotected, with the male image destroyed, the ordeal caused her to move from her psychological dependent state to a frozen independent state."

Willie Lynch

Black women have some serious problems and we must also blame the root of those problems on Willie Lynch. The modern day sister will have to confront the reality of how Mr. Lynch has successfully divided the black man from the black woman.

During slavery, an African male slave could be killed for standing up to the white man. Today, an African American man will suffer serious consequences for standing up to the institutions of the United States. The racist institutions of the United States of America are constantly dividing black women and black men.

Racism in the United States is a historical and modern day reality. Yes, even in our high tech world there is a continuous effort to keep African American women and men at odds with each other. Unfortunately, African American women easily fall for the trickery because they do not fully understand the power of the divide and conquer tactics.

Black women know they have to look out for themselves, but they also must understand most black men are victims of white supremacy!

Divide and conquer is the oldest game in the book of tricks. This is a reality African American women should not go though life denying. Relationships with their fathers, brothers, uncles, or any other black men have been affected by American racism.

There are a lot of black women who have "issues" and the root cause of some of their issues is the result of a poor or nonexistent relationship with their fathers.

Ask sisters - how many black men did they love and respect while they were growing up? Ask them if they have loving relationships with their fathers or uncles. How many African American women do you know who grew up seeing their parents interact in a loving manner? The point is many African American women did not have loving relationships with their fathers when they were children. This could be the reason why too many sisters have trouble understanding and loving African American men.

Now the world ain't perfect, so we should not think all of our relationships will be perfect. However, African American women will have better relationships with their "brothers" when they recognize, and then ignore the focuses that seek to divide black men and women.

There are differences between men and women, and these differences are exploited today. Most women tend to be a tad more emotional than men, but in most ways women are more focused and disciplined than the average man. This is one reason why so many black girls do so well in grade school, in college, and on the job.

People in power, who have the thinking of Willie Lynch, know women want security! Every woman wants to know the rent will be paid and her children will not go to bed hungry. In this country, if you do not have any money, you will quickly become homeless, hungry, and naked.

For most women, if not all African American women, money and security are the same! In today's world, an African American woman really does not need an African American man. At least not for any financial needs!

Not so long ago the slave owners had the money and the power. In modern day America, only a few brothers are multi-millionaires. There are some very successful athletes, entertainers, and businessmen, but they cannot compare to white male billionaires. Even the average brother cannot compare to the white male bosses on the job.

How many African America men have the money, and the power (meaning the security) a black woman truly desires?

Also, how many obedient, caring, loving, and wealthy brothers are there in the United States? An African American man who is wealthy and also a good listener is a fantasy for some African American women. In the real world, the sisters see too many black men standing on the corner, in front of a liquor store, or on the porch of their mama's house. Yes, there are millions of black men doing the right thing, but there are also millions of brothers who are losers.

African American women should understand that they are the ones who raised these un-ambitious, no good black men! African Americans mothers and grandmothers are famous for spoiling their boys. Too many well-intentioned black women let their little boys have their way and buy them too many toys and expensive clothes. These expensive clothes and toys give their boys a warped sense of reality. When the results of spoiling their boys become evident, there is no real plan to correct these poorly raised boys. Some of these African American boys grow up to be wild and disrespectful men with real character problems.

Women shouldn't spoil their boys just because there ain't no man in the house! They need to keep their boys off the mean streets and get them into wholesome activities that will build their character. African American children suffer from the lack of positive male role models. Children shouldn't raise themselves; so young African American mothers should ask "the village" to help them raise their boys and their girls.

Women are the first teachers of the children. If mom is uneducated or has no mother wit, what kind of children will she raise? Children are reflections of their parents. The apple does not fall far from the tree.

There is a disconnection between wise women and young foolish women. Wise, adult African American women have to get very real with African American girls while they are little girls!

A fifty-year-old young woman is wiser than a thirty-year-old woman. A thirty-year-old woman is wiser than a fifteen-year-old teen. There is far too much wisdom in the village for young women to make foolish choices because of a lack of knowledge.

We are surrounded by too much information for young women to continue to make poor choices. They need to know the real deal before they get into a situation they cannot deal with. Every girl should be culturally persuaded not to have any children in their late teens or early twenties. A young woman's youth is for learning and growing, not for raising children.

Child rearing is for the woman who has a plan and purpose for raising children.

The successful women of the village have to get real with our teen-age girls and share their knowledge. It's easy to bridge the generation gaps; Black women, just make it plain and tell these young women child rearing is an expensive and life altering experience! If you want to become poor, or remain poor, just have some children before you obtain a very good education!

Young women should be taught to love themselves and to stay away from men who will take advantage of their youth. Men will use our young women if our young women do not have high levels of self-esteem. There are plenty of brothers who will make babies with no plans to raise their own children. Young sisters beware!

The Willie Lynch's of the past and present have done a masterful job of dividing the African American woman from the African American man. In the 1970's, the welfare system would not provide assistance for the woman who lived with her man. In the 1980's the illegal drug culture exploded! Illegal drugs are purposely dumped into African American communities to destabilize them! Yes, the vast majority of African Americans say no to illegal drugs, but the drug culture that was set up by "the man" creates a great deal of chaos in African Americans neighborhoods.

Also, back in the 80's too many black women bought into that "I don't need no man" feminist-lesbian nonsense. Hopefully, the young sistas we have now will not fall for that trick.

Women love romance and fantasy so it is easy to trick them into not valuing the institutions of family and community. African American women have to be reminded that they are not white women.

Black women are also not white feminist. African American women are not white movie starlets or soap opera queens. African American women as a group will never attain the stature of white women. Black women are not the standard of beauty in the USA. When black women worked in the fields they could never become "Miss. Ann," but the supporting role of Aunt Jemima was available. The female slave was not on par with the master's wife or daughter.

During slavery, black women were field workers and servants for white people! During slavery, black women were raped and killed by white men. During slavery, a few black women were persuaded or forced to be the master's mistress. The job of mistress remains available today, and black women seeking money and status are still filling it.

Our reality is a reflection of our thoughts, and African American women have too many "I" thoughts. Too many sistas have selfish, "F--- the community, I'm looking out for me" thoughts. The goal of too many African American women is to earn a lot of money and spend a lot of money. Their goals rarely include having a father, (or father figures) in the lives of their children, or the uplifting of the African American community. It is all about me, not we, but me!

Black women do not fully understand Willie Lynch, African American men, and themselves in this modern time. There are millions of beautiful black women who are single because of Willie Lynch, television, movies, magazines, various fantasy books, and other deliberate forces.

African American women can think for themselves, but all too often enemy forces control their thoughts. There are a few conscious women, and they are vilified for being overly nationalistic or Afro-centric.

In the United States, money is valued and material wealth is valued, so African American men have very little value. In the minds of African American women, cash is king and many African American men are considered chump change! In America, a "good man" makes twenty thousand dollars a month, not twenty thousand dollars a year. A good man is a brother who lets his wife have her way. "Mr. Right" is a man who is wealthy, healthy, and obedient!

A whole lot of black women are waiting for Mr. Right, but Mr. Right ain't showing up. A sista will be waiting a long time for that fantasy brother who earns six figures. Now there are millions of average brothers who would be good mates! These are caring brothers earning twenty-five to sixty five thousand dollars a year.

Sorry sisters, you have to settle for less or settle for each other!

All African American women must come to a realization that the devaluation of the black man was started by our enemies and their goal is to weaken or destroy the influence and leadership of black men over the black family. We know the foundation of any civilization is the family, and a weakened family structure is disastrous to a people or a nation.

Black women should be very upset at Willie Lynch and also at today's institutional white supremacy, but they are not. Black women seem to only care about getting paid and spending money! So they are the consummate consumers and are no threat to the evilness that divides and conquers black people.

This is just one reason why African American women are promoted in American society over the African American man. It is because African American women will go with the flow even if three million African American men flow up the river to prison.

What a shame! African American women have the money to eliminate the economic poverty in our neighborhoods, but they would rather spend their money with people who do not believe in economic reciprocity. Some sisters have Koreans doing their nails, and Arabs doing their hair. Ain't that wild!

They especially love spending their money on expensive retail bullshit! African American women try very hard to buy their happiness, but at the end of the day, these sisters are left all alone with their expensive this and expensive that.

When will African American women wake up and realize they have been tricked? When will our mothers, grandmothers, and aunts realize Willie Lynch has tricked them? When will African American women realize they have the brainpower and the financial power to revitalize the economically depressed and morally depressed sections of the African American community?

Waiting on Jesus or hoping and praying the lost souls in the black community will eventually turn away from their wicked ways will not end the daily drama in our community.

BLACK MEN

"For fear of the young male's life, she will psychologically train him to be mentally weak and dependent but physically strong."

Willie Lynch

The brothers have some serious problems! Every day African American men have to fight a covert racist society and the negative perceptions and realities for just being black men. It's damn near a loosing battle! It takes a whole lot of energy to combat overt and covert racism . Only a few brothers are strong enough to deal with the mental stress and strain of white supremacy.

Too many brothers are not even aware of how white supremacy affects them. There are a whole lot of brothers that are angry and they take their anger out on their families. These men are physically beating up their girlfriends, their baby's mama, their babies, or their own mothers. There are thousands of young brothers terrorizing African American neighborhoods. They are angry, but they will not take their anger out on the "white man"!

These brothers do not have a historical awareness of institutional racism and white supremacy. We know it is not fashionable to blame "the white man," but white men have a long history of holding down the progress of the black man.

Please understand a conscious black man is a direct threat to the United States white male dominated society. The white man is a minority; he is only a small percentage of the earth's human population. He uses fear and ignorance to rule over the human family.

In the days of slavery, white men knew they had to turn their African slaves into something they could control. African men, women, and children were turned into Negroes. Today, most African American men are bourgeois Negroes, or ghetto Negroes; very few black men are attempting to raise the consciousness of the masses. The unseen forces don't want the masses to gain any awareness, so the manufacturing of men with a Negro or ghetto mentality continues to be a massive 24/7 process.

The modern African American boy is mentally crushed in grammar school. They may have some promise in pre-school or kindergarten, but in first grade the process kicks into high gear. By the time a boy gets to the sixth grade, the ballgame is almost over! African American boys need to be seriously protected from the brain washing tactics of the United States educational system. Black boys come out of grammar school not loving their African heritage, or themselves.

Year after year we allow our boys to attend inferior public schools and then we wonder why they don't like school. African American boys don't like school because the school educators, administrators, and the American educational system do not like African American boys.

The African American boys that are forced by their parents to conform to do well in school will tend to start acting "white." The boys who do not conform will tend to start acting like "niggers!"

For the sake of this argument, acting like white people means you have a dislike for the poor, or less educated African Americans. There is a real thin line between being educated and acting like white people. Children are not stupid and they know when a peer or adult is acting white. Children know when a teacher cares about them or when teachers are out for themselves.

How many formally educated African American men really care about the masses of African Americans?

Our boys need an excellent education, but they also have to be taught to love themselves. Boys who hate themselves can grow up to become men who abuse their girlfriends, wives, mothers, or grandmothers. A young man who loves himself is least likely to commit suicide or cause harm to his family or his neighborhood.

Some boys grow up to become well-adjusted men, and some boys grow up to become angry men. Special schools must be created for our "bad" boys. These grammar schools should be built in the country so the boys are far away from the angry urban life! Think about it! The United States government builds prisons in the country, but these institutions are there to make sure African American men never realize their true potential.

There are so many black men in prison that it would make a wise person think America's public schools and state prisons are structured to stop the rise of a black messiah. The powers that be do not want to see a modern version of Dr. Martin Luther King or Malcolm X.

Black men are about six percent of the United States' population and they are about fifty percent of the inmates in the various prisons throughout the United States.   African Americans are disproportionately in prison, disproportionately college dropouts, and they are disproportionately murdered. One can easily see there is a grand conspiracy to control or destroy young black men, thus destabilizing the black community.

The white man does not want to fairly compete with the black man on a mental or physical level. The black man is a very powerful human being. This is why the main goal of Willie Lynch was to separate the black man from the black woman. The black man is powerful and unstoppable when he works in unison with the black woman. Too bad the sisters and the brothers don't work together. Willie Lynch has bamboozled them.

Some African American men are physically threatening!   Some   African   American   men   are intellectually threatening! Some African American men are spiritually threatening! A brother who has his stuff together threatens the white man. There are plenty of successful African American men but the brothers have one strong weakness - women, especially white women!

There was a time when black men were killed for talking to, or just looking at, a white woman. Now jungle fever is a way of life. We know it's a challenge for any man to turn down some really good booty, but men can muster the energy to control themselves if they have real good reasons to control themselves.

Far too many African American men are focused on their personal needs and not the needs of the African American family. The white girls are focused on what they want and they know what black men want!

Most men have very simple needs. They want plenty of good food, good sports, and good sex! African American men want women to comfort them, not to constantly nag them! Sure, most men need to be aggressively encouraged, but not constantly nagged.

The white woman knows a man wants to be treated like a king, so she will do whatever it takes to make the black man feel like a king. Today, African American women have to compete with all kinds of women of color, and they must also compete with the black man's desire for a white woman!

The Brothers have a lot of issues, so they need wise Black women to help them focus on their family and not on frivolous activities.

The African American community has a chronic need for more African American families in our urban neighborhoods. We have too much chaos in our community because of the divisions between African American women and men.

Willie Lynch is still in effect! He did an outstanding job of getting us to distrust each other. It will take a few years of intense private meetings, community forums, and the mass production of culturally wholesome movies, television and radio shows to eliminate our Willie Lynch conditioning. The challenge is getting our well-read African American men to display some of their knowledge and creativity in public. These brothers need to quit "sciencing" to each other and go out and "science" to our African American boys!

Teaching our boys about their life in racist America is a formidable task but real men have to step in the ring and teach our boys how to triumph over the forces of evil. African American men and women have to let black men who are wise teach their boys the racist history of the United States and how present day America is still racist. We cannot expect the public school systems to teach black boys properly.

"The village" has to teach our boys principles and values. For far too long the African American community has allowed African American men to abandon their children. Unfortunately we can't teach old dogs, so we will have to focus our attention on our boys. They need to grow up in a community and culture that doesn't condone irresponsibility.

Children should have the love of their father or at least one healthy relationship with a real man. A boy will have trouble becoming a responsible man if he is allowed to be irresponsible, so it is our responsibility when the fathers are absent. Educators, preachers, athletes, and entertainers - all of us must help the young boys in our community become responsible men.

LEADERSHIP

"I have outlined a number of differences among the slaves, and I take these differences and make them bigger.   I use fear, distrust, and envy for control purposes."

Willie Lynch

The African American masses have a hard time unifying and transforming our low-income neighborhoods because of two forces - negroism and white supremacy.   We can defeat racism and white supremacy if we ever defeat negroism.

Unfortunately, most African American leaders act as if the white man cannot be defeated. The truth is, they really do not want white supremacy defeated. They will say, "How are we going to make some money without the help of the white man"? They have an "if you can't beat them, join them" mentality.

Many African American leaders pretend they are fighting for the advancement of the masses of black people, but they are really fighting for the advancement of themselves, their families, and their friends.   The original followers of Elijah Muhammad were taught about the 5% - the poor righteous teachers, the 10% - the bloodsuckers, and the 85% - the mentally dead masses. Most African American leaders would be tossed in the 85% group, but the rest are part of the 10% bloodsucking group. The 10% are people who have wisdom and knowledge, but use their wisdom and knowledge to hoodwink and bamboozle the African American mentally dead masses.

Too many African American leaders are corrupt to some degree. This is because they give in to the need to stay on top. That desire, combined with the desire to keep money rolling in, corrupts their honest intentions.

In the United States, the goal of most people is to make a whole lot of money and/or gain a whole lot of power. The goal of the poor is to just get through the day. The goal of the middle classes is to stay away from the poor people and to act like they have got it going on!

Living the life of the rich and famous is very exciting. Going to fancy parties, driving luxury automobiles, and living in a large home or a deluxe apartment in the sky is the goal of too many of our African American "leaders". In the United States, cash is king, and having a multi-million dollar investment portfolio is even better. This is especially true if you are a "leader". The poor masses will not follow someone poor like them, and the middle class will not follow someone who is not "educated".

The masses want their leaders to have lots of money, expensive cars, and fine clothes. The masses follow the "leader" or follow the follower rather than following proven principles and values. African

Americans follow truth mixed with falsehood, wrapped in dazzling packaging.

Most African American leaders probably feel the masses are asses! Because of this, many African American leaders face a dilemma. If they tell the masses of African Americans "the whole truth" the masses wouldn't believe it. If they told the masses the hard cold truth, they would lose their followers and go broke or get themselves killed. The truth can set the masses free, but it will also create some enemies for our leaders. The Willie Lynch powers that be don't want the black masses to know the truth, so the black leaders who know the truth keep it to themselves.

Any African American leader who tries to enlighten the masses will be vilified in the media. If that doesn't work, the IRS will investigate him or her. If that doesn't stop the bold black leader, the powers that be will find a way to put these black leaders in jail or have them killed!

New, strong, and truthful African American leaders are desperately needed to tell young African Americans about the Willie Lynch game. It is the game of divide and conquer! It has African Americans fighting and killing each other everyday.

There are white and black leaders who are running the Willie Lynch game on African Americans every day. The United States government, the media, and other American institutions are a part of the game. Young brothers and sisters need to know the United States has a history of investigating and infiltrating black organizations. If the United States had government agents and provocateurs in the past, they can surely have a counterintelligence program in effect right now.

There probably are investigations and infiltrations of black organizations going on right now, and their purpose is to keep us at odds with each other. Have you ever noticed that every time a group of African Americans begin to get a movement going some Negroes, or some conservatives, show up to derail the movement? Think about it!

African American communities are in chaos, and we are accustomed to chaos. Too many of our "leaders" believe the black poor have no intellect, so they just dazzle them with their bullshit. The truth is, the poor can be transformed if the culture around them changes.

New leaders are desperately needed to change our urban culture. We need new black leaders who are specialists. We need leaders who will specialize in finance, business, real estate, law, psychology, and education. These specialists have to show young African American students how run a business, and how to provide products and services for our black communities.

We also need black leaders that will take an issue and stay with it to the end. We will often see someone become very passionate about an issue for a month or a year, and then just burn out. Enlightening the masses is a hard job because the masses are comfortable. When you spend a lot of time listening to the radio or watching a silly TV show or DVD, you have very little time for enlightenment.

African Americans need leaders, but we do not need any more religious leaders. We have far too many religious "leaders"! We have prayed and turned the other cheek long enough! African Americans need at least 144,000 young hell raisers!

The problem with organized religion is that it is fear based, so it holds back African Americans from real enlightenment. Organized religion has the average brother and sister afraid of going to hell, but they must realize they are already living in hell. This is especially true if you are following a leader who is getting their "heaven on earth," while you live from paycheck to paycheck.

Many African American leaders are Christians, but they are afraid to truly become Christ like. Christ was a man of truth! He did not capitulate, grin and tap dance, or lick the boots of the Sadducees and Pharisees. Today's Christian ministers ought to be ashamed of themselves. How many ministers tell their followers that the kingdom of heaven is within? How many ministers tell their followers to work together, pool their resources, and turn their neighborhoods into a heaven on earth?

It would be wonderful if we had leaders that would enlighten us to the point where we did not need leaders.

African American leaders want the masses to follow them, but we need leaders that will lead the masses to themselves. The kingdom of heaven is within!

In this modern time, as we live in this new millennium, divisions still remain between the young and the old, the dark skin and the light skin, the male and the female African American. Our leaders should be working to end these divisions!

African Americans are a very confused people because real leaders are rarely allowed on major radio or TV talk shows. The media in America gives us African Americans who are non-threatening. When we see these brothers and sisters on television, they are very well read but they are conservatives or integrationists. The media producers keep the nationalist-thinking African American leaders far away from the masses (by keeping them out of the news media) for fear they will wake us all up.

It is all about mind control! It is all about controlling your thoughts! Who you are, where you live, and what you have, are all reflections of your thoughts. Willie Lynch conditioned the thoughts of the slaves and their thoughts were passed down from generation to generation. These are thoughts of fear, powerlessness, and distrust. You, the poor, the rich, or anyone else cannot become successful without the help of other people.

It takes a unified force of thought to bring thought into material reality. This is how an individual or a community manifests their goals. It takes real thinking, a real plan, a real purpose, and some real action to achieve a goal. Manifesting a thought from your mind into a physical reality may take some time, but it can be done. You have done this for yourself millions of times in your life. It may take months or years of positive actions before success is achieved in our communities, but success is inevitable for the person that is committed to the quest.

Fear is the number one reason for failure! That is why the assistance of wise people is definitely needed to overcome one's fears of failure. This is why leadership should encourage the masses of African Americans to think positive thoughts and work in a cooperative manner. Black leaders must teach the masses how to clear their minds and think with pure thoughts. If we had mind enlightening leaders, African Americans would be inspired to make every neighborhood safe and clean.

While we wait for the new leaders to emerge, it is up to ordinary people like you to lead the way. Yes, ordinary people like you! Your mission, if you choose to accept it, is to influence the influencers of popular culture. That means you have to call, write, e-mail, or go out in the streets and protest until you get their attention. Then tell the radio and television managers and the motion picture producers you want a positive depiction of Black people!

Let us examine today's dilemma. The civil rights generation got what they wanted and they are now on cruise control. Now the rest of us are like the children of Israel wandering in the wilderness. We will never get to the promise land until we make sure every African American neighborhood is safe, clean, and has excellent schools. We will quickly begin to achieve these goals soon after we come together and agree to attain these simple goals.

Yes, new young leaders are desperately needed!

RACE AND CLASS

"You must also have all your white servants and overseers distrust all blacks but it is necessary that your slaves trust and depend on us."

Willie Lynch

Old joke: What do you call a black man with a Ph.D. from Harvard? You call him or her nigger!

We hope this old joke is not a reality today, but African Americans as a group will never become equal to European Americans. Well, some whites will treat you as an equal if you do not show any real love for your people. Just become a race neutral Negro and you will have plenty of white friends!

Many economically successful African Americans have tried their best to become white, meaning they want to be accepted by whites. This is understandable, because white folks have all the money. The medium income African Americans have is half of the medium income of white Americans. This is one reason why most black neighborhoods don't look as nice as white neighborhoods. It takes a lot of money to keep a home looking like new. The other reason why most of our communities don't look as nice as other communities is African Americans have a love/hate relationship with each other.

Although we instinctively love each other, we were taught by Willie Lynch to distrust each other. This distrust is one reason why there are so many businesses run by other nationalities in our communities. When we see a black owned business, it triggers the thought, "Why should I make that nigger rich?" We become jealous and go spend our money with people who have no intentions of circulating money though the African American community. Most of the billions and billions of dollars we earn every year lands in banks, insurance companies, mortgage companies, and other business that are owned by European Americans.

We have all the money we need to solve all of our problems, but we spend too much money foolishly. We spend too much on the outside of our bodies vs. the inside of our bodies! We eat too much! We drink and get high too much! And of course, we gamble way too much money away! We buy millions of lottery tickets every day. You only need one ticket to win, but we buy 10, 20, or 30 tickets every week! The money we lose at the casino, the horse or dog track, and by buying lottery tickets adds up to hundreds of millions of dollars that could have been used to developed the minds of African American children.

African Americans also have love/hate feelings for whites and the United States of America. The United States is our home. We have lived here as a people for over four hundred years, and 95% of us have no intentions of moving back to the continent of Africa.

America has many problems, but it is the only home we know. Be it ever so racist, there is no place like home!

We are naturally peaceful people! We do not kill European Americans for the past and present unequal and genocidal treatment we have received. African Americans are like any other people, we just want peace, justice and equality. In America we have plenty of race and class issues. The lower educated African Americans have little class. The want-to-be bourgeoisie African Americans think they have a lot of class. The real, black bourgeoisies spend most of their time and money with their white classy friends.

In the good old USA, conservative African Americans are rewarded very well for being color blind Negroes. White conservatives accept this small group because they are non-threatening and would not dare blame Willie Lynch or any other European American for dividing black people. They act like there is no inequality and no injustices in the United States. They have been thoroughly brainwashed and see black as being bad and white as being good. African American conservatives believe the majority should rule, and white European Americans are the largest group of people in the United States.

African American conservatives may mean well, but they fail to realize they are pawns trotted out for the purpose of dividing African Americans. You may see black conservatives on television, but you will rarely see a black nationalist on the same TV show. The conservatives tell black folks to think for themselves and become successful individuals. Yes, anyone can become a successful individual in the USA. All you have to do is to use your education or skills to get a good job or open up a business. Give your customers or employers what they want, and then save and invest 10% of your earnings and live happily ever after. As an individual, you can achieve great success in America; but what about the rest of your people? The conservatives will tell you to forget about "your people"!

African Americans on the liberal side of the political spectrum ain't that much better! They spend too much time at some policy meeting, or at some political party, and not enough time on the ground with the urban poor. African American liberals are basically assimilationists, so they really do not want to solve the problems of the urban poor. Their focus is to keep their good jobs and keep on making money for European American corporations and foundations. African American politicians are assimilationists.

Today we have more elected officials and community organizations than ever before, but we know poverty and crime are still huge issues in our communities. African American Democrats and Republicans are not willing to (or are unable to) eliminate crime and poverty in the African American community. With the ineffectiveness of our politicians, we can understand why young Africans Americans and the poor don't vote. They don't see any real tangible results coming from the electoral process. What they see is African American liberals and conservatives being house Negroes who work in different parts of the master's house!

For younger African Americans, racism and white supremacy are like the atoms of the air. They cannot see it, touch it or smell it, but racism affects them every day of their lives. When they go to school, they're taught from a white American point of view. When they watch TV or go to the movies, they see the white European American worldview. When they go out and work in corporate America, they see American racism and capitalism in all its glory. When young African Americans find themselves in court, they are judged by white America's point of view. When the younger brothers and sisters finally figure out something ain't right, it's too late. It is a shame every generation is not sat down and taught all about the reality of the world.

Race and class issues are very real in the good old USA and the African American urban poor are burdened the most by it. Nobody wants to live with poor black people. In fact, poor black people do not even want to live in a poor black neighborhood. White families will live with black families until the black families begin to out number them.

The first fear of the white family is miscegenation! The slave master mixed his genetics with his black slaves, but the average white person doesn't want any race mixing. This is very understandable, and this needs to be thoroughly discussed. If you disagree, read this great book, <u>The Isis Papers</u>, by Dr. Frances Cress Welsing. The vast majority of European Americans live in European American neighborhoods. They do not want to live as a minority, surrounded by "the minorities". You can't fault them. They just need to be honest about their views on race relations in America.

It would be great to hear today's white parents say "I don't want my son or daughter having babies with black people." It would be great to hear today's white people say, "I am afraid of black people." Whites seem to fear retribution from African Americans. They seem to fear we will beat them up, or rob them, or have sexual relations with their women. We all need to begin speaking honestly about our feelings and about each other. This is natural; you would expect to see people of the same ethnic or racial group living in their own neighborhoods. Birds of a feather flock together.

However, there are some exceptions! Whether a community is homogenous or multicultural, we all know what goes on behind closed doors. Sexual attractions between men and women are natural, so we should expect more biracial children in the United States. There are some serious and uptight views about sexuality and race in the United States. All the different people in the United States must be honest about their feelings on race mixing. It is time for some new discussions on race in the USA. In the good old days, white Americans were the dominant race.

When we watched television shows or a movie in the past, we would see whites but very few African Americans, Latinos, Asians, or anyone else. Today's TV shows and movies have more "minority" actors but the whites are still the dominant race. This is the result of market forces and racist forces that are against the non-white people of America.

Remember, racism and capitalism go hand in hand. African Americans are rarely the leading men or women. If they are, they are Lone Rangers with a white Tonto as their sidekick. Also, there are not enough movies and TV shows where African Americans have a family, an extended black family, or black friends.

We are a very diverse group of human beings, and television producers do not want to show the diversity of today's African Americans. We all don't know each other. Some of us can't dance or sing, or run real fast. Either the white folks who produce television shows and motion pictures don't understand us, don't want to understand us, or they are totally focused on the bottom line. The majority of television and movie producers may not be racist, but there are probably a few whites in the media who can't stand black people.

We also know most white people have real trouble seeing the world the way we see the world. African Americans do not own the large media conglomerates, so we can only ask white folks to become fair and show the full spectrum of our life in America.

It is tempting to cut most whites some slack because they cannot really understand what it means to be an African American. Also, the average white person is not the real enemy. The average white person is striving to make a decent living for himself and his family. The real enemies of black people are the leaders and institutions of white American supremacy. The institutions of white America have created negative perceptions of African Americans and those negative perceptions are passed on to all Americans.

The perceptions are that black men are violent and sex crazy and black women are promiscuous and money hungry. Most Americans also think we all go to church on Sunday morning. They think everything black is bad and everything white is good. We have all bought into the constant vilification of African Americans by the media.

Racial problems remain real in America because American institutions are inherently racist. African Americans cannot get major motion pictures or television shows made without the approval of white people. African Americans cannot get a product on the shelf of a major store without the approval of white people. Basically, black people cannot do anything on a national or international scale without the approval of a white person.

Yes, white people control every aspect of capitalism in the United States. That's just the way it is! Every rich African American probably understands the white American power structure can make them poor overnight. The white man giveth and the white man can taketh away! Any brother or sister who forgets this racist, capitalist reality will be reminded!

Living in a racist society is bad, but being poor and living in a racist society is even worst. So, the American rich people keep their mouths shut. The middle class people keep their mouths shut, and the poor people continue in misery.

As a group, African Americans will never fully assimilate into mainstream American society. Capitalism cannot create equality! There will always be economic winners and losers under American capitalism. Regardless of the capital we have, only 10% to 20% of African Americans really want to fully assimilate into mainstream American society. Most of us want to maintain as much of our African American culture as possible.

White people are in power and we live in their world! They make the rules and change them whenever they feel like changing them. White people want to stay in control and they do so by making all the non-white people living in the "United" States of America accept their culture (and neglect their own cultures).

What is equally sad is that main line African American organizations continuing to strive for integration. Maybe soon these old civil rights organizations will realize they are at a dead end. Since

1865, whites have tried to tell African Americans they will not accept all of us. Liberal whites can only deal with a small percentage of us, and the white conservatives will only accept black folks who don't like being black. White people naturally prefer African Americans who are race neutral Negroes. They reject the Black Nationalist or the overly Afrocentric. Integration is all right for the rich or highly educated African American population, but white folks don't want the rest of us.

You would think it would be easy for African Americans to fully integrate into white communities since we are less than fifteen percent of the United States' population. Integration should be easy, right? The old civil rights generations wanted integration, or at least assimilation. They wanted European Americans to accepted them as equals. Fortunately the new generations don't have the same desires as their grandparents.

In the United States of America, there are lower income whites, Latinos, Asians, and other Americans. But the low income African Americans catch more hell then any other group. The United States of America has a real race and class problem. We tolerate each other because we have a few dollars in our pockets. As long as the money keeps flowing, we can all get along.

American society has always determined who is black and who is white. African Americans will quickly tell about their white bloodline, but you will rarely hear white people discuss their genetic history if it includes black blood. There is a new game "they" are playing to weaken the power of African Americans. The game is biracial allegiance and multiculturalism. Remember, their goal is to keep African Americans divided.

It does not matter what you call mixed race children, these children will have some hard choices. Who really wants to be black? In the USA, black is bad and white is good. America's media sets the standards for beauty and success. African Americans set the standards for athletics and entertainment, but we don't have the money and media power that white folks have. Because of this, most Americans strive for the European American's standards of success. Multiculturalism and biracial allegiance gives African Americans another way to distance themselves from our heritage as they strive to be "American". Hopefully, biracial African Americans will speak up and work for justice and equality for the black side of their families.

Believe it or not, there are some good white people. There are a few who fight for freedom, justice and equality. There are also a few we are friendly with on the job or at the ball game and who see African Americans as equal human beings. It is too bad there are only a few good white people in American with any real political or economic power. African Americans should work with them and other Americans of goodwill. However, the bulk of our time is needed in our own homes and communities.

THE FUTURE OF AFRICAN AMERICANS

"And he said unto Abram, Know of a surety that thy seed shall be a stranger in a land that is not theirs, and shall serve them; and they shall afflict them four hundred years; And also that nation, whom they shall serve, will I judge: and afterward shall they come out with great substance."
Genesis, 15th Chapter, Verses 13 and 14

The fate of African Americans is tied to the fate of the United States. Although the United States is changing, whites will stay in power because the American way is the white American way. Anyone who hopes to obtain any position of power must think like white European Americans. The future challenge for the powers that be is keeping the poor and lower educated African Americans happy in their neighborhoods or in prisons.

The "white man" has a great track record of conditioning and controlling the minds of African Americans. Television is the number one tool of mind control and African Americans watch more television than any people on the planet earth. TV distracts and pacifies black folks so well that we have little or no desire to improve the conditions in our urban neighborhoods.

The institutions in the United States have controlled the minds of the slaves, the Negroes, and today's African Americans.

When the United States was a developing country, black folks were slaves. Most of them did what they were told to do. After a few hundred years, we became sharecroppers! In the south and the north, most of us did what we were conditioned to do. When the United States went to war, African Americans went to fight for their country. African Americans have always been loyal servants to white people. Now that we are no longer loyal servants there is no real need for low income African Americans in the United States of America.

African Americans were present at the beginning of the United States and we will be present when the United States falls from grace. This is the place we call home. We don't know any better, or we don't think our lives can be any better living outside the United States.

Our minds have been programmed to believe that Jesus, or some other messiah, will save us before the United States goes down the drain. That would be wonderful. However, Jesus beaming African Americans up to heaven is against the physical laws of nature.

More than likely, the United States will continue its decline because the majority of its citizens refuse to be fair.   Capitalism, racism, and white supremacy have teamed up to beat down the majority of African Americans.   From the horrors of slavery up to the present, we have endured racism and white supremacy. When we moved from the south, racism was waiting for us in the northern cities.

When African Americans moved to the suburbs, racism was there to greet us.   Racism and white supremacy are everywhere. It is the American way.

At the founding of this great nation, white men owned slaves! For over two hundred years America has continued the great tradition of injustices and inequality. America has a long history and an ever-present reality of injustices and inequality against the Indians, the descendants of black African slaves, and anyone else who fights for real freedom and justice.

The modern day advocates for freedom and justice are not popular people. If you are against the American's unfair penal system, you're against the American way and conservative values. You are against white America if you are for justice for all; especially if you want justice for the descendants of black African slaves.

The United States' media will brand you a bonafied nut if you advocate the decriminalization of illegal drugs, or other consensual crimes. You will be considered a communist if you want a universal health plan for all USA citizens. In the United States there is freedom and opportunity, but your level of education and income limit your freedom and opportunities.

The United States is a good place to live for those who do not rock the boat, but all great governments eventually come to the end of the road. The United States of America can go in any of three directions. It could become a fair and just society. It could fall into a second world status. Or, it could totally collapse. We already see the economic gap between the rich and the poor widening. We are also seeing an expanding multicultural United States. We also see a defacto one world economic system. This is the natural progression of capitalism.

The United States is a country where you can see first world, second world, and third world communities. This is a country full of greatness and great contradictions. The United States is the land of milk and honey, and also a land like Sodom and Gomorra. There are mind blowing technical advances and also intense religious dogma, zealousness, and superstition. Eventually these contradictions will blow up into an intellectual battle.

We are beyond the year 2000 and real religious people continue to anticipate the arrival of a physical Jesus or some supreme messiah or unidentified flying objects coming down out of the sky to save the righteous.

We need to have some serious discussions about "the end of the world!" We need to ask the Hebrew Israelites if African Americans are really the chosen people of God. Also, the followers of Elijah Muhammad ought to fully explain the prophesy of Ezekiel's wheel in the sky. Is there a huge space station in the cosmos poised to destroy this the United States of America?

We also need to discuss the reality of Jesus! What parts of the Bible are real and what are the writer's parabolic embellishments? We should also study other religions and their visions for the end of the world. These questions are important because African Americans seem to be more focused on their life after they die as opposed to the life of their succeeding generations.

The majority of Americans would agree the end is near, but how near? The majority of Americans would agree the strange and aggressive weather that hits the United States is a sign. Is the strange weather a warning or is it the result of man made chemicals altering the earth's atmosphere?

All good and bad things must come to an end, so let's analyze the present. Can the United States of American remain the earth's number one super power as it becomes more and more multicultural? Will the United States go through a steep economic decline, a devastating military defeat, or diplomatic blunder that will allow the European Union to become the Earth's "one world" super power? When will World War III begin? Will it be in 2017, 2027, or 2037?

What is the war of Armageddon? Is it a final battle between Christianity vs. Islam? Is the war of Armageddon a final war between White people vs. the earth's people of color? If there is a God, the final punishment of the wicked is inevitable. It may be too late for the guilty to repent.

The United States government has not yet given reparations for slavery. They have not given apologies for the past and present ill treatment of African Americans. Please understand that some religious people believe African Americans are like the Hebrew slaves and God will punish the United States!

White people are a minority on the planet so you will see them continue to concentrate their power to maintain their power. They will also continue to give up some power to stay in power. Don't be surprised when you see a Latino Pope, or a Pope of African decent. Don't be surprised when you see a female President and an African American President. You may see this within the next fifteen to twenty-five years. However, it doesn't matter who is the front man or woman, the white man will always be in charge!

The United States is the number one economic super power for now, but it looks like the European Common Market is poised to take that position. Whether the United States remains the ruler of the free world or slides back to second or third place really doesn't matter. Some time in this century, white people will have to earnestly share power with the earth's people of color.

This will happen after their spears are turned into plow shears and they study war no more.

In present day America, it's about money, and the love of money could eventually ruin the United States of America. The love of money can create evils and selfishness. The power of the military, world trade, and the willingness of national and international investors back the USA dollar. If the United States totally collapses, the world's economic systems will also collapse. If the United States falls, African Americans will go down the drain with everyone else! In the meantime and for the foreseeable future, African American civil rights organizations will continue to rant and rave about how we are not treated like wealthy white Americans.

The deeply and semi-religious African Americans will continue to wait on Jesus or some other messiah to beam them up to heaven. The rest of us will enjoy life in the moment by watching TV, spending money, gambling, shaking our booty, stuffing our faces, getting high, or getting our freak on. Ninety five percent of black people will continue to do what they have been doing.

With all this mirth and merriment going on, we will see a small group of African Americans who will make preparations to go back home! This sounds crazy, but many African Americans have moved to Africa and we will see more brothers and sister leave the United States. It sounds crazy now, but American capitalism cannot last forever. Now if you feel the United States is doomed, go get your reparations and start making preparations to leave the country.

The new world order will get old real fast, and the nations of Asia and the Arab world may end up having a world war with the United States and Europe. You cannot persuade black people to leave America even if there was a threat of World War III, the economic collapse of the United States, or any other disaster you can think of.

At the end of slavery, most of the slaves did not want to go back to Africa because North America was the only home they knew. Most African Americans feel like Americans, not Africans. Moving to Africa is a scary proposition.

In reality, only a very small percentage of African Americans will eventually move to the continent of Africa because they will become extremely dissatisfied with America. The millions that remain will continue to be second, third, and fourth class citizens. They will continue to fight the white power structure for civil rights and equality.

Most African Americans believe in a Supreme Being. They feel their personal problems and the world's problems will receive a divine solution. African Americans need to believe that they are divine, **and that they are the Gods that will solve all of their problems!**

African Americans have the power and money to solve every problem facing us today. We just suffer from the curse of Willie Lynch. We are blinded and stymied by envy, jealousy, and distrust of each other.

The more things change, the more they stay the same. That's an old, trite, saying but it's true for African Americans. At the turn of the last century, whites had total control in the United States and we suffered injustice and inequality.

Today, white Americans continue to control the United States and we suffered injustice and inequality. The descendents of African slaves seem to be content with their lives in the United States. Or, we are so overwhelmed with life's daily struggles we have very little energy to fight the forces that divide and conquer.

There are millions of African Americans who are dissatisfied with their lives in America, but there are not enough young leaders to organize them. The Marcus Garvey movement flourished in the 1920's; hopefully we don't have to wait long for history to repeat itself!

DIVIDE AND CONQUER!

"Don't forget, you must pit the old black male vs. the young black male, and the young black female against the old black female."

Willie Lynch

The Willie Lynch's of the past and present has victimized African Americans. Yes, African Americans are victims of European American's racism. Being a victim is not the problem. The challenge today is to rally to overcome the effects of the oppression we have suffered. Now that is a real challenge!

Do you think a person that can't read (or doesn't read) has the intellect needed to ignore the forces of deception? There is an old saying, "If you want to keep something from a nigger, put it in a book!" Not enough African Americans read books for the purpose of improving the quality of life in our communities. There are books and websites that will help anyone get more out of life. There is plenty of "how to" information - how to find a good husband, raise smart children, run a successful business, and successfully invest money.

Of course, history books and biographies are some of the best books to read. Books on the history of Africans in America are filled with stories of triumph over racism.

White folks have always made it hard for black folks to achieve. But when the playing field is even (and many, many times when it is not), black people achieve! After our talented brothers and sisters become successful, they are socially separated from the masses of black people. Thus, we do not fully benefit from their talents, money or intellect.

We don't all look alike or think alike, and we don't all have the same goals and aspirations. However, we all have a common history and we should not forget our ancestors who suffered though the centuries of slavery and the hellish years after slavery. Despite our education, economic, or political differences, African Americans must work together to end the crime and poverty in our neighborhoods.

This book is for everyone to read, but especially for African American teens and young adults. They will have to decide whether to remain in the United States of America or relocate somewhere on the continent named Africa. The thought of leaving the United States wouldn't be necessary if America was a place of peace, justice, and equality. The USA is a great place to live if you have the money to stay away from crime-ridden neighborhoods. The poor in America have very few options. The poor endure the majority of the injustices of the United States. It is up to the upper and middle income African Americans to protect their less successful brothers and sisters. This is dammed near impossible because we are so divided and conquered. Willie Lynch did a great job of pitting the black woman against the black man, and the old against the young, and the light skin slaves against the darker skin slaves. Today we remain distrustful of each other and bridging the gaps between the different economic classes is our biggest challenge. Today our talented, our best and our brightest educated brothers and sisters are used to benefit white folks, not us!

African Americans must come to gripes with reality and step out of the troubled waters of denial. Yes, it is time for African Americans to blame "the white man" for most of our problems! After we get that off of our chest, then we can begin to take responsibility for our future. It is time for African Americans to end the curse of Willie Lynch!

Mr. Lynch was right! His tactics have lasted for 300 years. It is amazing African Americans have been mental slaves for so long! We act like we don't want to be free. We act like we just want to have a good time and we do not care about justice and peace enough to work together for it. Instead, we just want large amounts of pleasure and all the things rich white folks have. It's as if we want to buy our way to happiness. The way we think and what we do is no accident because we have been programmed to be mental slaves by Willie Lynch.

This is our life in the United States of America, the land of the free and the home of the slaves!

CONCLUSION

This book was written to stimulate thought, create some debates, and inspire some action! It was also written with the hope that this book would be a small part of a new cultural movement. We need a movement that will insure that every African American neighborhood is safe and clean with excellent schools.

It does not matter if we live in the city, the suburbs, or in a small southern town, a new movement is needed to end the effects of Willie Lynch! The civil rights era basically ended with the assassination of Dr. Martin Luther King Jr. The civil rights organizations of today are self-aggrandizing. They don't concentrate their efforts on making our old urban neighborhoods safe for women and children. They are only concerned with getting jobs and contracts for themselves, their family and a few close friends.

Too many middle class African Americans have been living off the success of the civil rights movement. As the civil rights generation ages, the post civil rights generation has the responsibility of improving the quality of life in African American communities. We can make life better for our children and grandchildren by organizing our mental and monetary resources. It is time to "circle the wagons" and pool our resources and protect our children.

Elijah Muhammad was the last leader that showed African Americans how to pool their resources. Since the years of the old Nation of Islam, African Americans have been wandering in the wilderness. It may take a few more years before the Hip-Hop generation develops a new push for a resources movement, but this movement is inevitable.

It is about time African Americans finally removed the mental shackles of slavery. We have the talent, and the money, but do we have the desire? If we started now, we would see improvements in one year, and great changes three years.

Now you are probably asking yourself, "How? What can I do today to begin to solve the societal ills of the African American community? How can I end the ignorance and the selfishness among African Americans?"

If you want to do something, just physically or financially support a positive youth program in your neighborhood. The main challenge facing African Americans living in low-income neighborhoods is providing positive male role models for our children. If we just did that, most of our other challenges will take care of themselves! It is actually easy to improve the conditions of urban Black Africa. Just send some money today to an organization that teaches young people wholesome values and principles.

The Public Schools in the United States have a middle class education model that presumes all students have loving parents that booster their self-esteem, instill discipline, and reinforce academic skills.

A new education plan is needed for the students who suffer from a poor self-image, who lack discipline, and who lack academic support at home.

Walk by a public school in your neighborhood and you see a lot of students who need some love, attention, and an after school program. A cultural movement is desperately needed to save the next generation of African American children.

You would probably agree African Americans cannot exactly recreate a Marcus Garvey movement, or Dr. Martin Luther King's civil rights movement, and we are too Christian to follow all the teachings of Elijah Muhammad. However, we need to reexamine the writings and speeches of these great men.

Mr. Muhammad said white people are naturally devilish people who make mischief all over the world. Christianity teaches its followers to love their enemies and to turn the other cheek. Do you think we will ever see a Black Nationalist Christian?

African Americans should also follow Booker T. Washington's advice and lower our buckets. We have all the money we need right in our own neighborhoods.

We need more electricians, carpenters, and other people with skills to perform services for each other. It is a shame we have to ask other nationalities to fix our houses and our cars.

It would also be wise for African Americans to modernize and expand W. E. B. Dubois' vision of the talented tenth. African Americans receive college degrees every year. More brothers and sisters need to resist the temptations of the white life and use their education to build businesses that will benefit African Americans. All of us want to live in clean and safe neighborhoods with excellent schools, but evidently some African Americans feel they cannot stop the crime in our neighborhoods.

Leadership is desperately needed to inspire all the different tribes in the African American communities to work together to make their neighborhoods safe and clean. When a new wave of leaders emerges, make sure you ask them if white people finance them!

African Americans should be suspicious of leaders and organizations that receive thousands of dollars from American corporations. African Americans must finance the organizations of our new young leaders. We do not want our young leaders corrupted by large sums of white money.

The suspicion and tension between blacks and whites will never end. White people have a long history of wars and rumors of wars. Genocide is also part of their history. Privately, African Americans feel AIDS is a virus created to kill undesirable human beings. By undesirable human beings, we mean poor people and especially people of color in Africa and Asia. Mother earth can provide the resources needed to feed, clothe, and shelter every human being, but the rich and super rich have no plans to care for all of Gods children.

Although there is obvious injustice, inequality, and genocide, African Americans should not waste any energy hating the white people we see every day. Our focuses should be on transforming crime-ridden and economically depressed African American neighborhoods. We should concentrate on strengthening our families and providing excellent educations for our children. After we save ourselves, then we can go save the rest of the world!

Whether we choose to live the rest of our lives in the United States, or choose to follow the path of W. E. B. Dubois and move to the west coast of Africa, we must continue to focus on our families, our schools, and our communities. When African Americans eliminate the crime and poverty in our urban neighborhoods, we will gain the respect of the world. Our goal must be simple – it must be to have clean and safe neighborhoods with excellent schools so our children can excel!

We should not allow ourselves to be distracted by any wars, any media subterfuge, or by the reparations movement. It is ok to participate in the reparations movement, but do not let it distract you from making our neighborhoods clean and safe for African American women and children.

The reparations movement is very necessary, but it could divert us from pooling our resources right now so we can solve all our challenges. It may take twenty to twenty-five years of consistent pressure on the United States government for the descendants of African slaves to obtain reparations for slavery.

The next step is to watch out for the Negroes leaders who will try to water down the final settlement. As the reparations for slavery fight goes on, our Willie Lynch slave mentality has to be destroyed before we are qualified to receive our forty acres, a mule, and millions of dollars from the U.S. government.

If every African American received a million dollars today, we would see far too many of us go on a mad spending spree and thus giving all the money back to white people. First we have to get our act together. This means we must end the Willie Lynch mind set before we can correctly handle any reparations! African Americans must take responsibility for our successes and failures in our communities.

We should not hold any animosity against Latinos, Asians, or any other new immigrants. They have been allowed to immigrate to the United States so whites can benefit from their labor and their income. Only large numbers of black people are not wanted in the United States of America. The European American powers have always sought to control, incarcerate, or kill black people. The purveyors of the Willie Lynch plan were so successful at brain washing their slaves that the descendants of African slaves cause as much harm to themselves as their former slaver owners did.

The resurrection of the mentally dead is long over due! When will African Americans wake up?

The entire world is waiting for African Americans to wake up and take control of their minds. In the past, when black people began to wake up, Negro leaders were dispatched to rock black people back to sleep. The next time African Americans begin to smell the coffee, the agents and provocateurs will not be so successful. With computer technology so widely available, and so easy to use, everyone can read and understand the Willie Lynch speech. The flow of mind enlightening information is unstoppable!

A person has really got to go out of their way to remain ignorant. There are bookstores, libraries, talk radio, 24 hours of TV news, informational audiotapes and compact discs to listen to in your car or wherever you are. Only a deliberate fool would consciously reject undeniable truth. Soon and very soon, even a fool will not be able to tell that lie "I did not know."

AFTERWORD

"Be not afraid, only believe."
Mark, Chapter 5:Verse 36

When I was a boy, back in the 1970's, I wanted to play baseball for the Chicago White Sox. I had daydreams of hitting homeruns, and doing my home run trot as the huge scoreboard explodes fireworks in to the Southside sky.

Dick Allen played first base for the White Sox. He was my favorite ball player. He wore the number 15, my lucky number. It would have been great to play professional baseball at the old White Sox Park!

I had daydreams and daydreams of playing right field. There were deep fly balls, and I would back up on the warning track, stick my out my hand to feel the closeness of the outfield wall. At the last second I would leap up and make a spectacular catch.

My dreams of a baseball career ended thirty years ago after one season of little league. I thought I wasn't good enough to play pony league and play for my high school baseball team. I was also far too afraid to leave Chicago and try out for a minor league team.

Although I never achieved my baseball dreams I did taste a bit of baseball glory. The night the White Sox clinched a division title in 1983 I was there.

The old White Sox Park was packed, standing room only! The Sox hadn't won anything since 1959 so this night was magic for Sox fans. When the final out was made the massive crowd exploded! The force of the crowd seem to push me down the stairs of the right field stands, then over the green padded wall, and down on to the warring track. There was pandemonium on the field! I was running a run on the outfield as fire works filled the Chicago sky!

I tell you this story to remind you that your mental visions can become a reality. Maybe not exactly they way you envisioned, but your mind can draw you to your goals.

In grammar school and in high school I daydreamed of being a news anchor for the CBS owned TV station. I would sit at my desk and mentally pretend I was anchoring the Channel 2 News.

I wanted to give Chicagoans my views on the news. I had big dreams, but no plans to make them a reality. High school quickly ended and so did my daydreams of becoming a TV news anchor. The dream faded because I was afraid. I lacked the academic skills, the discipline, and the confidence to prepare myself to be a news anchor.

Fear prevented me from asking anyone for wisdom and guidance. I suffered from a very poor self-image.

Eleven years later I mustered enough positive energy to become a public access producer. This wasn't anchoring the Channel 2 News, but millions of Chicagoans could watch me provide information that they could not get on commercial television. The core of my life long dream became a reality and I hoped my cable TV show would become a part of a cultural movement that will that insure that every African American neighborhood would be safe, clean, and have excellent public schools.

During the 1970's I wondered why Black people would intensely signify on each other. Why were we calling each other Black Sambos, high yellow niggas, and other degrading names? I wanted to know why some Black people lived in "the ghetto"? Why was it that everything white was good and everything black was bad? Today you and I know the truth, but there are billions of people on earth who do not have a clue, or are in deep denial.

Part of my mission in life is to "demystify the bullshit", and enlighten the masses! What is your mission in life?

Staying focused and achieving your personal goals are almost impossible without having a mission. The forces of evil will knock you down, but you cannot allow theses forces, your fears and any lack of confidence to keep you down. It is easy to give up, but you can't give up! Hang in there, use whatever skills you have, never quit, and you will succeed.

You have the responsibility of inspiring and nurturing future generations. The children you see everyday have dreams and goals, and it is our responsibility to help them achieve their goals.

We all have goals, dreams, and desires, but fear stops most people from living a more productive life. My fears have delayed this small book from being written and published. It has taken me more than ten years to overcome the fear of criticism. Some fears are natural, but most are learned, and all fears are in the mind. Fear is preventing the masses of African Americans from living a life far beyond a paycheck-to-paycheck existence. African Americans think it is impossible to end the pervasive crime and hopelessness in our low-income neighborhoods. However, all things are possible! We can achieve our goals as soon as we get over our fears.

Yes, I am talking about our conscious and unconscious fears of criticism, loss of friendship and loss of employment. Overcoming these fears are not an easy task, for "the White man" controls for every aspect of life in the United States of America. During slavery Black people were punished for opposing white supremacy and today African Americans are afraid to oppose the racist institutions of the United States.

We have been conditioned to fear and admire the local and national institutions of the United States of America. We are conditioned to revere these institutions as children, to the point where most people are brainwashed for life.

African Americas will serve and protect the racist institutions of the United States before even mildly considering serving and protecting each other. Black people are subconsciously afraid of White people!

Systematically we have been made afraid to be our natural selves, and conduct our selves in a royal manner. Yes, we are royalty, we are the sons and daughters of God!

Everyday we kill each other in our neighborhood, or kill other human beings all over the world for the US military, but we know we better not harm any White people here in the United States! Consciously and subconsciously all African Americans know it is not wise to take on "the Man", his institutions or his family! We have been boxed in by "the Man" and his Black Bourgeoisie minions, who the "the Man" has trained to be our "leaders."

Integration has made us totally dependent on the benevolence of European Americans. Most of our jobs, mortgages, insurance, business loans and consumer loans all come from white folks!

We are like a third world nation placed in check by debt and dependency.   You can speak out against inequality, injustice, and white supremacy, but at your own economic peril!   There are a few economically free African Americans but they are shamefully too full of fear to speak against white supremacy.

One reason this book was written was to free the author from "the master's plantation." Slavery ended a long time ago but, African American employees and many African American owned businesses depend on a modern day "massa" to throw us some pork.

I could have run away to freedom at anytime but was fearful I could not survive without a paycheck.   A steady paycheck can defer the dream of becoming self-employed.   Freeing yourself from debt and dead-end jobs is an extremely daunting task!   Very few people can free themselves from their fears all by themselves. There are African Americans who have freed themselves from the plantation, but how many of them are leading other black people to freedom?

You may have great dreams, desires, and goals but are afraid to go down the rough road to freedom.

To free your self from your fears, your neurosis, your character disorder, or any other mental challenges you have may take years of dogged determination.   Then again, you could begin the process of transforming yourself today!

Everyday there are "moments of truth" where we choose to take a positive or negative action.

You can allow irrational fear to control you and stifle your personal growth or you can become proactive and move closer to achieving your goals! I know it is hard to overcome fear, but you can. You have overcome other fears in the pass, and you can overcome your current fears in an instant. I hope this book has inspired you to take some action today that moves you closer to achieving your goals.

I wrote the first part of the book years ago, then became discouraged and stopped. A few years went by before I was inspired to finish this book. Then there was two years of rewriting and proofreading. During the entire process there were hours, days, weeks, and months of procrastination.

This small book is the result of a transformed self-image. For years and years I felt I was not smart enough to write a book. I felt I was not smart enough to go beyond a paycheck-to-paycheck existence.

Most African Americans are in a perpetual survival mode. They are held down by the vicious forces of racism, classism, self-doubt, superstition, and religious dogma. These are pretty strong forces to overcome, but theses mental chains can be broken! A cultural movement is desperately needed to improve the self-image of the masses of Black people.

I am sure you have heard the naysayers lament; "It is hopeless"! "Trying to wake up the children of the mentally dead masses is a waste of your valuable time!" "Black people don't want freedom, they want fantasy!" "Why are you trying to push a mule that does not want to move?" "Forget about the poor, and focus on making yourself one of the rich!"

These are the worlds of the naysayers, but just imagine African Americans working together and ending the crime and poverty that plagues our lower income neighborhoods. When we achieve this seemingly impossible dream, half of the world would ask us for wisdom and guidance.

We are approaching the end of the world! Not the end of the planet earth, but the end of wars and rumors of wars. We are witnessing the fulfillment of "the scriptures" and the end of the bamboozlement of the masses! There is too much wisdom and technology for this world to have famine, diseases, and explicit ignorance. It is the responsibility of the righteous to enlighten and empower the masses, but the forces of evil frightens most of the righteous, so they stick their heads in the sand. Which leaves them wide open for a good kick in the butt!

There is only a very small percent of "really" bad people in a high crime neighborhood. These people lead their minions to do evil and scare the rest of us back into our homes. Who are these people? Where did they come from? Are they evil spirits, or government agent provocateurs?   These evil spirits who make our neighborhoods "bad" are our children!

Black people are naturally peaceful people.   It is unnatural for us to distrust, disrespect, and commit crimes against each other.   There is an evil element that influences African American culture, our thoughts, and our consciousness.

The system of white supremacy is very real and our children must be aware of it. Our children, especially our boys must know the "white man" is out to get them! The US government has, and will place agent provocateurs in African American neighborhoods to destabilize them.   Don't you wander why we cannot work together to pool our resources and fund afterschool, and Saturday school programs for all our children?

If there is a group of African Americans trying to organize to improve the conditions in our lower income neighborhoods, you best believe Negro provocateurs will be sent in to derail the process.   We could negate these Negroes and end the chaos in our community if we focus on our children. Some children are blessed with a loving, nurturing home to go to after school.

There also millions of African American children who ain't so lucky.   If we really loved all children we would provide programs and instructions that will help them with their homework and inspire them to become productive human beings.   The main thing that is stopping us is Willie Lynch. It is time to end the Willie Lynch effect!

Willie Lynch is a metaphor for the divide and conquer tactics that are used on Black people. Remember, the goal of our enemies is to keep the Black man, the Black woman, and their children divided! It is time to end our ignorance of the world we live in, and our self-hatred of each other.

There are six billion people on the earth but only a hundred and forty four thousand are needed the transform urban Black American and the rest of the world.

This is where "the tipping point" meets "the six degrees of separation". This is how ideas can enter the consciousness of millions, or billions of people. This is how thoughts manifest into material things.

There were only a small percent of Black people who directly participated on the civil rights movement; a "movement" that influenced the entire world!

One committed person can influence thousands of people, and a small group of committed people can influence millions! We all have a circle of influence. We all know two or three hundred people. Also, every one we know knows at least two or three hundred people.

Good news travels fast, and bad news even faster. There are positive and negative thoughts all around us.

You have the power to send positive thoughts throughout the entire universe!

Do you think it is possible to raise the awareness of Black people to the point where we do not tolerate street crimes and inferior public schools?

Let me repeat, the goal is to make every African American neighborhood safe and clean, and to provide excellent schools for our children.

A cultural movement is the best way to achieve this goal. The goal must be repeated again and again until it is ingrained the minds of the masses of Black people. This can be accomplished via the institutions and celebrities that influence popular culture.

This process of transforming urban Black America begins with you sending positive information to your circle of influence. You may not personally know any athletes or entertainers, but the people you know have friends or family that knows someone that personally knows someone who influences popular culture.

When you contact everyone you know, you are connecting with thousands, maybe millions of people. Do you think a phone call, letter, post card, e-mail, or a thought saying "be not afraid, only believe" would positively influence almost everyone you know? Can you think of some other thought, message, or idea that would positively influence almost everyone you know?

Will you consider sending positive thoughts to everyone you know?

All things are possible, but we must believe all things are possible. We will have all the power we need to transform our community if we only believe we have power.

Too many of us believe there will always be homes and neighborhoods filled with chaos and drama. We can end the chaos and drama, but we need to replace our thoughts of complacency and hopelessness with thoughts of a transforming power and a divine purpose.

# # #

THE END

Dear Friend:

If you purchased this book I very sincerely thank you.

Your patronage allows me to provide complimentary copies for teenagers.

*If you are an adult and you received a complimentary copy, I encourage you to purchase a copy of **Willie Lynch: Why African Americans Have So Many Issues** for a young adult.*

This book was especially written for teens and twenty year olds. The decisions they make today will greatly impact their future.

The more knowledge and wisdom our young people have, the better decisions they will make. **The more knowledge and wisdom you have will greatly determine your future.**

I do not expect young people to agree with my opinions, **I just want them to expand their thinking.**

Feel free to contact me. **I want to hear your opinions on the future of African Americans.**

Sincerely,

Marc Sims
P.O. Box 5415
Chicago, IL. 60680
Willielynch2013@yahoo.com

PS: If we do not remove the Willie Lynch noose around our necks, African Americans will soon become null and void.

5 Reasons Why Many African Americans live in poverty:

1.   Racism
2.   Negroism
3.   Destabilized families
4.   Bad public schools
5.   Lack of fiscal prudence

The purpose of this book is to encourage African Americans to intensely focus on ending the crime and violence that plagues many of our low-income neighborhoods.

First, we must stop having babies in our teens and early twenties!

Second, we must stop going on mad spending sprees, and invest our money for financial independence.

The goal is to insure every African American neighborhood is safe and clean, with excellent schools.

The goal is to end the ghetto mentality.

We do this by teaching our children all about Willie Lynch, and the history of racism in the United States.   **Digital audio and video media is the best way teach our children.**

Negroism:
The belief that educated African Americans are superior to other African Americans.
The belief that integration and/or assimilation is the best way for African Americans to succeed in the USA.

Required Reading

The Mis-education of the Negro
Carter G Woodson

Message to the Black Man
Elijah Muhammad

The Isis Papers
Dr. Frances Cress Welsing

The Blackman's Guide to Understanding the Blackwoman
Shaharazad Ali

Autobiography of Malcolm X
Alex Haley

The Philosophy and Opinions of Marcus Garvey
Amy Jacques Garvey

Raising Black Children: Two Leading Psychiatrists Confront the Educational, Social and Emotional Problems Facing Black Children
James P. Comer, Alvin F. Poussant

Whatever Happened to Daddy's Little Girl?
The Impact of Fatherlessness on Black Women
Jonetta Rose Barras

Additional Recommended Reading

Passport to a Happy Marriage
Abdul Alim Bashir

Toms, Coons, Mulattos, Mammies & Bucks:
An Interpretive History of Blacks in American Films
Donald Bogle

The Lost Cities of Africa
Basil Davidson

The Souls of Black Folk
W.E.B. DuBois

Family Roots
Mildred El-Amin

Black Skin, White Mask
Franz Fanon

The Fire Next Time
James Baldwin

A Salute to Black Scientists and Inventors
Robert Hayden

Countering the Conspiracy to Destroy Black Boys
Jawanza Kunjufu

Black Men, Obsolete, Single, Dangerous?

Haki Madhubuti

World's Great Men of Color
J.A. Rogers

Black Chicago, The Making of a Negro Ghetto
Allan Spear

Race First: The Ideological and Organizational Struggles of Marcus Garvey and the Universal Negro Improvement Association
Toni Martin

Black Folks Guide to Business Success
George Subira

They Came Before Columbus
Ivan Van Sertima

The Psychopathic Racial Personality
Dr. Bobby E. Wright

Why Blacks Kill Blacks
Dr. Alvin Poussaint

Black Students, Middle Class Teachers
Jawanza Kunjufu

Sisters Helping Sisters
Madeleine Wright

God, The Black Man and Truth
Ben Ammi

Before The Mayflower
Lerone Bennett

Toms, Coons Mullattos, Mammies and Bucks: An Interpretive History of Blacks in American Films
Donald Bogle

Black English
J.L. Dillard

Roots: The Saga of an American Family
Alex Haley

Black Anglo Saxons
Dr. Nathan Hare and Dr. Julia Hare

Where Do We Go From Here: Chaos or Community
Dr. Martin Luther King, Jr.

The Black Bourgeoisie

Black Priest/ White Church
Father Lawrence E. Lucas

The American Directory of Certified Uncle Toms
Council on Black Internal Affairs

The Head Negro in Charge Syndrome
Norman Kelley

**Dictionary of the Principles of Misconduct
in the Workplace**
Clarence C. Terry

The Black Church in the African-American Experience
C. Eric Lincoln

Is Bill Cosby Right?
Michael Eric Dyson

PowerNomics
Claud Anderson

The Autobiography of Black Jazz
Dempsey Travis

**We Have No Leaders:
African-Americans in the Post-Civil Rights Era**
Robert Smith

Black Lies, White Lies
Tony Brown

"Dirty Little Secrets" About Black History
Claud Anderson

Black Labor, White Wealth
Claud Anderson

The Jewish Phenomenon
Steven Silbiger

**Any book at a Black Book Store
****Any book from the African American section of the
    library**

Notes

Notes

Notes